Quilt by Color

SCRAPPY QUILTS WITH A PLAN

Susan Ache

Martingale®
Create with Confidence

Quilt by Color: Scrappy Quilts with a Plan
© 2019 by Susan Ache

Martingale®
19021 120th Ave. NE, Ste. 102
Bothell, WA 98011-9511 USA
ShopMartingale.com

Printed in China
24 23 22 21 20 19   8 7 6 5 4 3 2 1

Library of Congress Cataloging-in-Publication Data is available upon request.

ISBN: 978-1-68356-027-2

MISSION STATEMENT

We empower makers who use fabric and yarn to make life more enjoyable.

CREDITS

PUBLISHER AND CHIEF VISIONARY OFFICER
Jennifer Erbe Keltner

CONTENT DIRECTOR
Karen Costello Soltys

MANAGING EDITOR
Tina Cook

ACQUISITIONS AND DEVELOPMENT EDITOR
Laurie Baker

TECHNICAL EDITOR
Nancy Mahoney

COPY EDITOR
Durby Peterson

DESIGN MANAGER
Adrienne Smitke

PRODUCTION MANAGER
Regina Girard

COVER AND BOOK DESIGNER
Kathy Kotomaimoce

LOCATION PHOTOGRAPHER
Adam Albright

STUDIO PHOTOGRAPHER
Brent Kane

ILLUSTRATOR
Christine Erikson

SPECIAL THANKS

Photography for this book was taken at the homes of Tracie Fish (Instagram: @fishtailcottage) of Bothell, Washington, and Libby Warnken of Ankeny, Iowa.

Contents

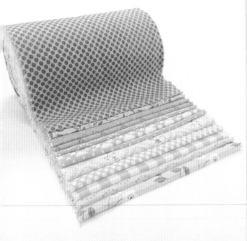

WHAT'S A
Color Cut?

Color Cuts are bundles of 12 fabrics, curated by color schemes. You can buy Color Cuts in ½-yard bundles, fat-quarter bundles, 5"-strip bundles (called dessert rolls), or 10"-square bundles. Each bundle contains 12 different prints in a similar color. And there are many color options: Sprout (greens), Beach Glass (aquas), Sugar on Top (whites), Road Trip (grays), Daybreak (pinks), Biscotti (creams), Indigos (dark blue), and many more.

Color Mine Scrappy

Just when you think you've seen every type of precut fabric imaginable, along comes something different and exciting. If you love color as I love color, you're going to adore the Color Cuts fabrics from Moda. Rather than bundling precuts of all the fabrics in one designer's line, Moda has combined prints from various designers into bundles curated solely by their colors. Genius!

So if you spend time wondering if these reds go together or if those blues are too different to "match" in a scrap quilt, Color Cuts will eliminate the doubt. Rolled into one bundle, they all work together brilliantly. The work is done!

I love that I can buy a bundle of fabrics labeled "Gingerbread" or "Sugar on Top" or "Biscotti." (Are you getting hungry yet?) If the names of the collections aren't enough to make you salivate, this will: each bundle of Color Cuts fabric gives you enough variety to make your next project scrappy—even if you don't have a fabric stash.

In this book you'll find patterns for nine quilts, along with beautiful photos of each. And all of them were made with bundles of Color Cuts. If you already have a big stash to choose from, don't worry—I've also given yardage requirements. And if you want to start with Color Cuts, I tell you which specific ones I used. Feel free to use the same, or mix it up and choose your own colorways. There are so many options to choose from.

Now that you know what Color Cuts are, you can imagine how much fun they are to play with. You can mix and match them for an instantly scrappy quilt because you start with not one blue, but 12. Not one light print for the background, but 12. See how easy it is to build a stash or create a scrap quilt?

I'll let you in on a little secret. The plan was to make eight quilts for this book. But once I had these Color Cut fabrics in my hand, I couldn't stop myself and I made an extra one. We were able to squeeze all nine quilts into this book, so get ready to make the scrap quilt (or two or three) of your dreams!

~Susan

Kaleidoscopic

FINISHED QUILT
57" × 70⅜"

FINISHED BLOCK
8" × 8"

*O*h boy, do I love a Kaleidoscope quilt! Have you ever looked at the actual quilt and tried picking out the block? Well, I have, and I love the look of the single block that makes up that cool design of an overall kaleidoscope. Strip piecing and using just one background fabric makes for some pretty fast work.

Materials

Yardage is based on 42"-wide fabric.

2 yards of ivory print for blocks and setting triangles

1 strip, 2½" × 42" *each,* of 9 assorted aqua and teal prints for blocks*

1⅜ yards of red check for sashing and binding

½ yard of red print for sashing squares and inner border

1⅞ yards of aqua print for outer border

3½ yards of fabric for backing

63" × 77" piece of batting

Template plastic

For the aqua and teal prints, I used Beach Glass Color Cuts in the Dessert Roll size (5" x 42").

Cutting

All measurements include ¼" seam allowances.

From the ivory print, cut:

3 strips, 3¼" × 42"; crosscut the strips into 36 squares, 3¼" × 3¼". Cut the squares in half diagonally to yield 72 triangles.

9 strips, 2½" × 42"

3 squares, 14¾" × 14¾"; cut the squares into quarters diagonally to yield 12 side triangles (2 are extra)

2 squares, 8¾" × 8¾"; cut the squares in half diagonally to yield 4 corner triangles

From the red check, cut:

12 strips, 2" × 42"; crosscut into 48 rectangles, 2" × 8½"

7 strips, 2½" × 42"

From the red print, cut:

8 strips, 2" × 42"; crosscut *2 strips* into 31 squares, 2" × 2"

From the aqua print, cut on the *lengthwise* grain:

2 strips, 6" × 59⅜"

2 strips, 6" × 57"

Making the Blocks

Press all seam allowances in the direction indicated by the arrows.

1. Join ivory and aqua 2½"-wide strips along their long edges to make a strip set. Make nine strip sets measuring 4½" × 42", including seam allowances.

Make 9 strip sets, 4½" × 42".

2. Trace the wedge pattern on page 11 onto template plastic and cut out the template on the drawn line.

3. Position the template on a strip set, with the wide end of the template aligned with the raw edge of the aqua strip. Use a ruler and rotary cutter to cut along both edges of the template to release the wedge shape.

4. Rotate the template 180° and position it with the wide end aligned with the raw edge of the ivory strip. Cut along both edges of the template to release the wedge shape. Repeat to cut a total of eight wedges from each edge of each strip set (144 total).

5. Lay out four wedges with aqua bottoms and four wedges with ivory bottoms, all cut from one strip set as shown. Sew the wedges together into pairs. Join the pairs to make two block halves. Then join the halves, matching the seam intersections. Sew ivory triangles to the corners of the block. Make 18 blocks. Trim the blocks to measure 8½" square, including seam allowances.

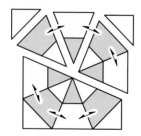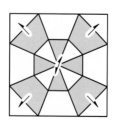

Make 18 blocks,
8½" × 8½".

Assembling the Quilt Top

1. Lay out the blocks, red check rectangles, red print squares, and ivory side triangles in diagonal rows as shown in the quilt assembly diagram below. Sew the pieces together into rows. Join the rows, adding the ivory corner triangles last.

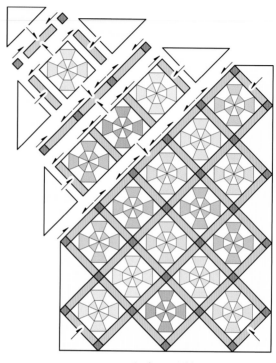

Quilt assembly

2. Trim the quilt top to measure 43" × 56⅜", including seam allowances, making sure to leave ¼" beyond the points on all of the squares for seam allowances.

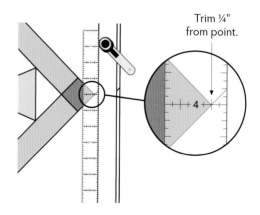

Trim ¼"
from point.

KALEIDOSCOPIC

3. Join the red print strips end to end. From the pieced strip, cut two 56⅜"-long strips and two 46"-long strips. Sew the longer strips to opposite sides of the quilt top. Sew the shorter strips to the top and bottom of the quilt top, which should measure 46" × 59⅜", including seam allowances.

4. Sew the aqua 59⅜"-long strips to opposite sides of the quilt top. Sew the 57"-long strips to the top and bottom of the quilt top, which should measure 57" × 70⅜".

Adding borders

Finishing the Quilt

For more details on any finishing steps, visit ShopMartingale.com/HowtoQuilt for free downloadable information.

1. Prepare the quilt backing so it's about 6" larger in both directions than the quilt top.

2. Layer the quilt top with batting and backing; baste the layers together.

3. Quilt by hand or machine. The quilt shown is machine quilted with an allover design of swirls and circles.

4. Use the red check 2½"-wide strips to make the binding; attach the binding to the quilt.

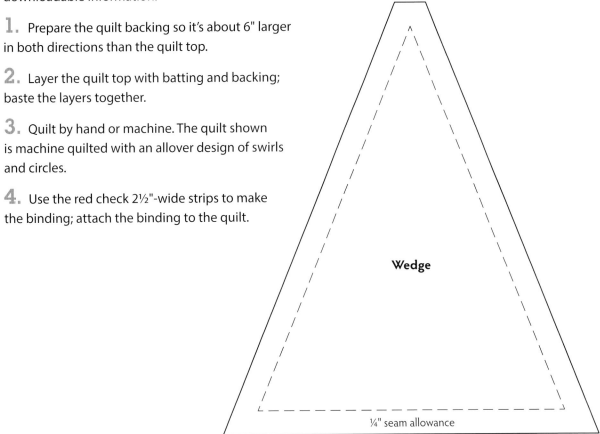

Wedge

¼" seam allowance

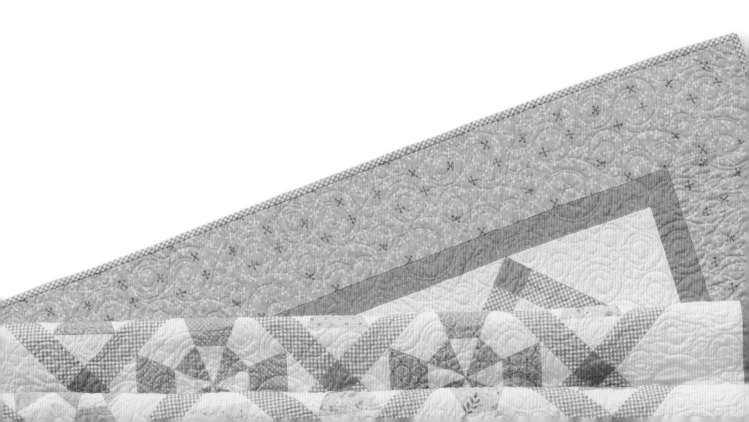

Fiesta

FINISHED QUILT
62½" × 62½"

FINISHED BLOCK
14" × 14"

Not sure who started Taco Tuesday, but as far as I'm concerned, it could be every day of the week and I would be happy. I just made my Tuesday table more festive with the addition of Fiesta. And I think you might like the fact that I made sewing this quilt a bit more fun by using some great tools. (See my tips on pages 14 and 17.) If you haven't tried Moda Crossweave, it's the perfect shade of black to give bright Color Cuts a happy fiesta touch.

Materials

Yardage is based on 42"-wide fabric. Fat eighths measure 9" × 21".

2¾ yards of white print for blocks, sashing, and outer border

1¾ yards of black print for blocks, sashing, and inner border

5 fat eighths of assorted dark or medium pink prints for blocks and sashing (collectively referred to as "dark")*

5 fat eighths of assorted light pink prints for blocks and sashing*

⅝ yard of yellow print for blocks and binding

7 fat eighths of assorted yellow prints for blocks and sashing*

4 fat eighths of assorted blue prints for blocks and sashing*

4 fat eighths of assorted green prints for blocks and sashing*

3⅞ yards of fabric for backing

69" × 69" piece of batting

Bloc Loc flying-geese ruler (optional)

In place of the assorted pink, yellow, blue, and green fat eighths, you can use the Color Cuts Dessert Roll Assortment, which includes all of these colors plus gray and white prints.

Cutting

All measurements include ¼" seam allowances.

From the white print, cut:

2 strips, 3½" × 42"; crosscut the strips into 18 squares, 3½" × 3½"

11 strips, 3" × 42"; crosscut *5 strips* into 62 squares, 3" × 3"

7 strips, 2½" × 42"; crosscut the strips into 108 squares, 2½" × 2½"

8 strips, 2¾" × 42"; crosscut the strips into:
32 rectangles, 2¾" × 4¾"
48 squares, 2¾" × 2¾"

1 strip, 4½" × 42"; crosscut the strip into 4 squares, 4½" × 4½"

Continued on page 14

Continued from page 13

From the black print, cut:

2 strips, 3½" × 42"; crosscut the strips into 18 squares, 3½" × 3½"

5 strips, 3" × 42"; crosscut the strips into 60 squares, 3" × 3"

1 strip, 2½" × 42"; crosscut the strip into 9 squares, 2½" × 2½"

7 strips, 2¾" × 42"; crosscut the strips into:
  24 rectangles, 2¾" × 4¾"
  48 squares, 2¾" × 2¾"

6 strips, 2" × 42"

From *1* dark pink fat eighth, cut:

2 strips, 2½" × 21"; crosscut the strips into 16 squares, 2½" × 2½"

2 squares, 3" × 3"

From *each remaining* dark pink fat eighth, cut:

2 strips, 2½" × 21"; crosscut the strips into 12 squares, 2½" × 2½" (48 total)

1 rectangle, 2½" × 4½" (4 total)

From *1* light pink fat eighth, cut:

1 strip, 2½" × 21"; crosscut the strip into 8 squares, 2½" × 2½"

From *each remaining* light pink fat eighth, cut:

3 strips, 2½" × 21"; crosscut the strips into:
  5 rectangles, 2½" × 4½" (20 total)
  8 squares, 2½" × 2½" (32 total)

From the yellow print for blocks and binding, cut:

8 strips, 2½" × 42"; crosscut *1 of the strips* into 16 squares, 2½" × 2½"

From *each of 3* yellow fat eighths, cut:

2 strips, 2½" × 21"; crosscut the strips into 16 squares, 2½" × 2½" (48 total)

From *each remaining* yellow fat eighth, cut:

2 strips, 2½" × 21"; crosscut the strips into 11 squares, 2½" × 2½" (44 total)

From *each of 2* blue fat eighths, cut:

2 strips, 2½" × 21"; crosscut the strips into 16 squares, 2½" × 2½" (32 total)

2 squares, 2¾" × 2¾" (4 total)

From *each remaining* blue fat eighth, cut:

2 squares, 2¾" × 2¾" (4 total)

4 squares, 2½" × 2½" (8 total)

From *each of 2* green fat eighths, cut:

2 strips, 2½" × 21"; crosscut the strips into 16 squares, 2½" × 2½" (32 total)

2 squares, 2¾" × 2¾" (4 total)

From *each remaining* green fat eighth, cut:

2 squares, 2¾" × 2¾" (4 total)

4 squares, 2½" × 2½" (8 total)

Triangle Paper for Fiesta

I like to use half-square-triangle paper to get perfect units. For this quilt, I used seven sheets of Moda Cake Mix Recipe 3. Instead of cutting white and black 3" squares, I cut seven white and seven black 10" squares. If you choose this method, skip step 1 of "Making the Blocks" and follow the manufacturer's instructions to make a total of 126 half-square-triangle units. You'll have six units left over for another project. Note that you will still need to cut two white 3" squares for step 2 on page 16.

FIESTA

2. Repeat step 1 using the remaining marked white squares and the dark pink 3" squares to make four half-square-triangle units measuring 2½" square, including seam allowances. Set the units aside for assembling the quilt top.

Make 4 units,
2½" × 2½".

3. Repeat step 1 using the white and black 3½" squares to make 36 half-square-triangle units. On the wrong side of one of the units, draw a diagonal line from corner to corner, perpendicular to the seamline. Place two units right sides together. Make sure contrasting fabrics are facing each other and the marked square is on top. Nest the diagonal seams against each other and stitch ¼" from both sides of the marked line. Cut the units apart on the drawn line to make two hourglass units. Make 36 units. Trim the units to measure 2½" square, including seam allowances.

Make 36 units.

4. Lay out one yellow square, eight matching yellow squares from a different print, eight black/white half-square-triangle units, 12 matching blue 2½" squares, 12 white 2½" squares, two different light pink squares, one dark pink square, four hourglass units, and one black 2½" square in seven rows as shown. Sew the squares and units together into rows. Join the rows to make a block measuring 14½" square, including seam allowances.

Repeat to make a total of nine blocks, referring to the photo on page 15 and the quilt assembly diagram

Making the Blocks

Press all seam allowances in the direction indicated by the arrows.

1. Draw a diagonal line from corner to corner on the wrong side of the white 3" squares. Layer a marked square on a black 3" square, right sides together. Sew ¼" from both sides of the drawn line. Cut the unit apart on the marked line to make two half-square-triangle units. Make 120 units. Trim the units to measure 2½" square, including seam allowances.

Make 120 units.

on page 19 for color placement guidance as needed. Set aside the remaining black/white half-square-triangle units for sashing units.

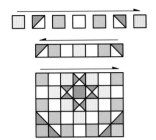

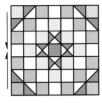

Make 9 blocks,
14½" × 14½".

Making the Sashing Units

1. Draw a diagonal line from corner to corner on the wrong side of the black 2¾" squares. Place a marked square on one end of a white rectangle, right sides together. Sew on the marked line. Trim the excess corner fabric ¼" from the stitched line. Place a marked square on the opposite end of the white rectangle. Sew and trim as before to make a flying-geese unit. Make 24 units. Trim the units to measure 2½" × 4½", including seam allowances.

Make 24 units,
2½" × 4½".

Trim the Flying-Geese Units

I used a Bloc Loc flying-geese ruler to trim the units to the exact size needed for this quilt. Wow, what a difference it made using a tool of the trade!

2. Draw a diagonal line from corner to corner on the wrong side of the white 2¾" squares. Place a marked square on one end of a black rectangle, right sides together. Repeat step 1 to make 24 units.

Make 24 units,
2½" × 4½".

3. Draw a diagonal line from corner to corner on the wrong side of the green and blue 2¾" squares. Place a marked square on one end of a white rectangle, right sides together. Sew and trim as before. Place a matching square on the opposite end of the rectangle. Sew and trim to make a flying-geese unit. Make four green and four blue units. Trim the units to measure 2½" × 4½", including seam allowances.

Make 4 of each unit,
2½" × 4½".

4. Draw a diagonal line from corner to corner on the wrong side of four matching blue 2½" squares. Place marked squares on opposite corners of a white 4½" square. Sew on the marked line. Trim the excess corner fabric, ¼" from the stitched line. Place marked squares on the remaining corners of the square. Sew and trim as before to make a square-in-a-square unit. Make two green and two blue units measuring 4½" square, including seam allowances.

Make 2 of each unit,
4½" × 4½".

Assembling the Quilt Top

Refer to the photo on page 15 and the quilt assembly diagram on page 19 for placement guidance as needed throughout.

1. On a design wall, lay out the blocks in three rows of three blocks each. Place the black/white flying-geese units between the blocks, making sure the black triangles form diamond shapes. Place a square-in-a-square unit in the center of each diamond shape. Place the black/white half-square-triangle units around the perimeter, making sure the black triangles complete the diamond or half-diamond shapes. Add the green and blue flying-geese units.

2. Pin four light pink rectangles to each corresponding block on the design wall. Pin light pink rectangles and squares along the top and bottom edges. Pin dark pink rectangles along the side edges. Add the appropriate blue, yellow, green, and dark pink squares to the edges of each block. Place two yellow squares and one pink/white half-square-triangle unit in each outer corner. Make sure that the pieces around each center star and square-in-a-square unit all match.

3. When you're pleased with the layout, join the black/white flying-geese units, print squares, and pink rectangles to make sashing unit A. Make 12 units that measure 4½" × 14½", including seam allowances. Return each unit to the appropriate position in the quilt layout.

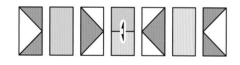

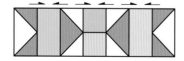

Sashing unit A.
Make 12 units,
4½" × 14½".

4. Join four black/white half-square-triangle units and three print squares to make sashing unit B. Make 12 units that measure 2½" × 14½", including seam allowances. Return each unit to its appropriate position in the quilt layout.

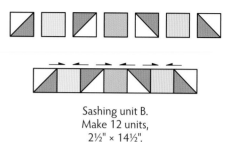

Sashing unit B.
Make 12 units,
2½" × 14½".

5. Join two pink/white half-square-triangle units, three B sashing units, one green flying-geese unit, and one blue flying-geese unit to make the top row. The row should measure 2½" × 54½", including seam allowances. Repeat to make the bottom row.

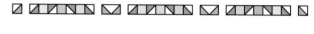

Make 2 rows,
2½" × 54½".

6. Join two A sashing units, three blocks, and two B sashing units to make a block row. Make three rows that measure 14½" × 54½", including seam allowances.

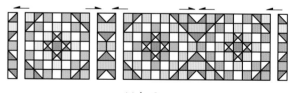

Make 3 rows,
14½" × 54½".

7. Join one green flying-geese unit, three A sashing units, one green square-in-a-square unit, one blue square-in-a-square unit, and one blue flying-geese unit to make a sashing row. Make two rows that measure 4½" × 54½", including seam allowances.

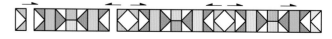

Make 2 rows,
4½" × 54½".

8. Join the rows from steps 5–7 to complete the quilt-top center. The quilt top should measure 54½" square, including seam allowances.

Adding the Borders

1. Join the black 2"-wide strips end to end. From the pieced strip, cut two 57½"-long strips and two 54½"-long strips. Sew the shorter strips to opposite sides of the quilt top. Sew the longer strips to the top and bottom of the quilt top. Press all seam allowances toward the black strips. The quilt top should measure 57½" square, including seam allowances.

2. Join the white 3"-wide strips end to end. From the pieced strip, cut two 62½"-long strips and two 57½"-long strips. Sew the shorter strips to opposite sides of the quilt top. Sew the longer strips to the top and bottom of the quilt top. Press all seam allowances toward the white strips. The quilt top should measure 62½" square.

Finishing the Quilt

For more details on any finishing steps, visit ShopMartingale.com/HowtoQuilt for free downloadable information.

1. Prepare the quilt backing so it's about 6" larger in both directions than the quilt top.

2. Layer the quilt top with batting and backing; baste the layers together.

3. Quilt by hand or machine. The quilt shown is machine quilted with an allover puzzle design.

4. Use the yellow 2½"-wide strips to make the binding; attach the binding to the quilt.

Quilt assembly

Blue Diamonds

FINISHED QUILT
57½" × 73½"

FINISHED BLOCK
12" × 12"

What happens when you've saved a perfect blue stripe for ages and suddenly find yourself with green Sprouts Color Cuts? Well, you immediately go and hunt for some pretty blues to match your perfect stripe and make a quilt. Fresh is the word to describe this color combo.

Materials

Yardage is based on 42"-wide fabric. Fat eighths measure 9" × 21".

2½ yards of cream floral for blocks, sashing, outer border, and binding

18 fat eighths of assorted green prints for blocks and sashing*

1⅝ yards of cream print for blocks and sashing

⅞ yard of blue-and-white stripe for block corners

10 fat eighths of assorted blue prints for sashing

½ yard of green print for inner border

3⅝ yards of fabric for backing

64" × 80" piece of batting

In place of the assorted green fat eighths, I used the ½-yard bundle of Sprouts Color Cuts.

Cutting

All measurements include ¼" seam allowances.

From the cream floral, cut:
7 strips, 2½" × 42"

From the remaining cream floral, cut on the *lengthwise* grain:
2 strips, 5½" × 63½"
2 strips, 5½" × 57½"
3 strips, 2½" × length of fabric; crosscut the strips into:
    10 rectangles, 2½" × 4½"
    48 squares, 2½" × 2½"
4 strips, 1½" × length of fabric; crosscut the strips into:
    36 rectangles, 1½" × 4½"
    36 rectangles, 1½" × 2½"

From *each* green fat eighth, cut:
5 rectangles, 2½" × 4½" (90 total; 8 are extra)
1 square, 2½" × 2½" (18 total)

From the cream print, cut:
20 strips, 2½" × 42"; crosscut the strips into:
    48 rectangles, 2½" × 4½"
    212 squares, 2½" × 2½"

From the blue stripe, cut:
6 strips, 4½" × 42"; crosscut the strips into
    48 squares, 4½" × 4½"

From *each of 6* blue fat eighths, cut:
1 square, 4½" × 4½" (6 total)
4 rectangles, 2½" × 4½" (24 total)

From *each remaining* blue fat eighth, cut:
3 squares, 4½" × 4½" (12 total; 1 is extra)

From the green print for inner border, cut:
6 strips, 2" × 42"

Making the Blocks

Press all seam allowances in the direction indicated by the arrows. In the quilt shown, blue stripes run horizontally in all but two blocks. The instructions have been simplified for ease of construction.

1. Sew cream floral 1½" × 2½" rectangles to opposite sides of a green square. Sew cream floral 1½" × 4½" rectangles to the top and bottom to make a center unit. Make 18 units measuring 4½" square, including seam allowances. Twelve are block centers and six are for sashing squares (see step 1, page 24).

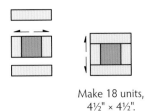

Make 18 units,
4½" × 4½".

2. Draw a diagonal line from corner to corner on the wrong side of 144 cream print 2½" squares. Place a marked square on the upper-left corner of a blue stripe square. Sew on the marked line. Trim excess corner fabric ¼" from the stitched line. Place marked squares on opposite corners of the blue stripe square. Sew and trim as before to make a corner unit. Make 24 units measuring 4½" square, including seam allowances. Make 24 mirror-image units.

Make 24 of each unit,
4½" × 4½".

3. Join a cream print 2½" × 4½" rectangle and a green rectangle along their long edges to make a side unit. Make 12 sets of 4 matching units (48 total) measuring 4½" square, including seam allowances.

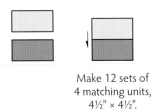

Make 12 sets of
4 matching units,
4½" × 4½".

4. Lay out four corner units, four matching side units, and a center unit in three rows, rotating units as shown. The green print should match in the side and center units. Sew the units together into rows. Join the rows to make a block. Make 12 blocks measuring 12½" square, including seam allowances.

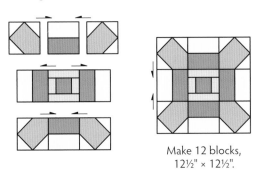

Make 12 blocks,
12½" × 12½".

Making the Sashing Units

1. Draw a diagonal line from corner to corner on the wrong side of the cream floral 2½" squares. Place a marked square on one end of a blue rectangle, right sides together. Sew on the line. Trim the excess corner fabric, ¼" from the seam. Place a marked square on the opposite end of the rectangle. Sew and trim as before to make a flying-geese unit. Make six sets of 4 matching units (24 total). The units should measure 2½" × 4½", including seam allowances.

Make 6 sets of
4 matching units,
2½" × 4½".

23
BLUE DIAMONDS

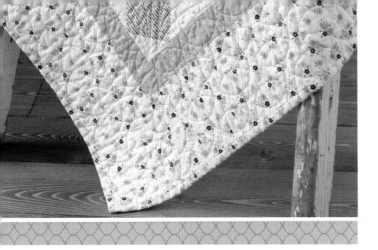

rectangle next to each square-in-a-square unit and then add a cream floral rectangle.

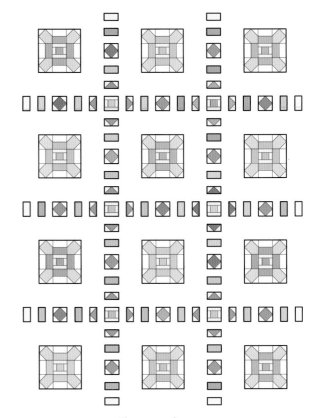

Placement diagram

2. When you're pleased with the arrangement, join one cream floral rectangle, two green rectangles, one square-in-a-square unit, and one flying-geese unit to make sashing unit A. Make 10 units that measure 4½" × 12½", including seam allowances. Return each unit to the appropriate position in the quilt layout.

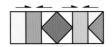

Sashing unit A.
Make 10 units, 4½" × 12½".

3. Join two flying-geese units, two green rectangles, and one square-in-a-square unit to make sashing unit B. Make seven units that measure 4½" × 12½", including seam allowances. Return each unit to the appropriate position in the quilt layout.

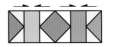

Sashing unit B.
Make 7 units, 4½" × 12½".

2. Draw a diagonal line from corner to corner on the wrong side of the remaining cream print 2½" squares. Place matching squares on opposite corners of a blue print 4½" square. Sew on the marked line. Trim the excess corner fabric, ¼" from the stitched line. Place matching marked squares on the remaining corners of the square. Sew and trim as before to make a square-in-a-square unit. Make 17 units measuring 4½" square, including seam allowances.

Make 17 units,
4½" × 4½".

Assembling the Quilt Top

Refer to the photo on page 23 and the quilt assembly diagram on page 25 for placement guidance as needed throughout.

1. On a design wall, lay out the blocks in four rows of three blocks each, leaving 5" between blocks. Pin the sashing squares from step 1 of "Making the Blocks" between the blocks for sashing corners. Pin four matching flying-geese units around each sashing corner. Pin four matching green rectangles around the flying-geese units, making sure the green print is the same as in the sashing square. Pin a square-in-a-square unit between the green rectangles. Around the perimeter, pin a green

4. Join three blocks and two A units to make block row A, which should measure 12½" × 44½", including seam allowances. Repeat to make block row C, making sure to rotate the A units as shown in the quilt assembly diagram.

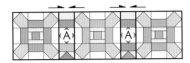

Row A.
Make 1 row, 12½" × 44½".

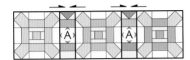

Row C.
Make 1 row, 12½" × 44½".

5. Join two A units, two sashing corners, and one B unit to make a sashing row. Make three sashing rows measuring 4½" × 44½", including seam allowances.

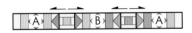

Sashing row.
Make 3 rows, 4½" × 44½".

6. Join three blocks and two B units to make block row B. Repeat to make a second row. Rows should measure 12½" × 44½", including seam allowances.

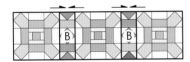

Row B.
Make 2 rows, 12½" × 44½".

7. Join the block and sashing rows from steps 4–6 as shown in the quilt assembly diagram to complete the quilt-top center. The quilt top should measure 44½" × 60½", including seam allowances. Press the seam allowances toward the sashing rows.

Adding the Borders

1. Join the green 2"-wide strips end to end. From the pieced strip, cut two 60½"-long strips and two 47½"-long strips. Sew the longer strips to opposite sides of the quilt top. Sew the shorter strips to the top and bottom. Press all seam allowances toward the green strips. The quilt top should measure 47½" × 63½", including seam allowances.

2. Sew the cream floral 63½"-long strips to opposite sides of the quilt top. Sew the cream floral 57½"-long strips to the top and bottom. Press all seam allowances toward the cream floral strips. The quilt top should measure 57½" × 73½".

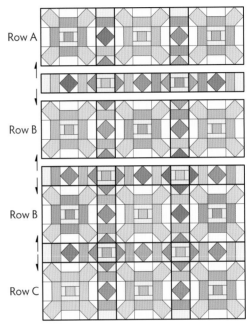

Quilt assembly

Finishing the Quilt

For more details on any finishing steps, visit ShopMartingale.com/HowtoQuilt for free downloadable information.

1. Prepare the quilt backing so it's about 6" larger in both directions than the quilt top.

2. Layer the quilt top with batting and backing; baste the layers together.

3. Quilt by hand or machine. The quilt shown is machine quilted with an allover design of curved and straight lines in the quilt center. The borders are quilted with a continuous egg-and-dart design.

4. Use the cream floral 2½"-wide strips to make the binding; attach the binding to the quilt.

Scrap Call

FINISHED QUILT
59½" × 70½"

FINISHED BLOCK
9" × 9"

Y ou betcha I have favorite prints, and you can be sure that they will always wind up somewhere in a scrap quilt. My go-to, never-without background color is Moda Bella Solids Ivory.

This is one quilt that I could make again and again in different colors and backgrounds. Keep it simple or make it scrappy, or even make it a holiday quilt. Play with your favorites and you'll have your very own version of Scrap Call.

Materials

Yardage is based on 42"-wide fabric.

3⅝ yards of ivory solid for blocks, border, and binding

¼ yard *each* of 30 assorted prints for blocks and sashing corners*

1⅓ yard of aqua solid for sashing

3¾ yards of fabric for backing

66" × 77" piece of batting

In place of the ¼-yard cuts of 30 assorted prints, I used an assortment of Color Cuts Dessert Rolls in aqua, green, gray, yellow, and pink prints.

Cutting

All measurements include ¼" seam allowances.

From the ivory solid, cut:
10 strips, 3" × 42"; crosscut the strips into
    120 squares, 3" × 3"
34 strips, 1½" × 42"; crosscut the strips into:
    30 strips, 1½" × 25"
    120 rectangles, 1½" × 4½"
14 strips, 2½" × 42"

From *each* of the assorted prints, cut:
1 strip, 1½" × 42"; crosscut the strip into:
    1 strip, 1½" × 25" (30 total)
    5 squares, 1½" × 1½" (150 total)
4 squares, 3" × 3" (120 total)

From the aqua solid, cut:
13 strips, 2½" × 42"; crosscut the strips into
    49 rectangles, 2½" × 9½"
6 strips, 1½" × 9½"; crosscut the strips into
    22 rectangles, 1½" × 9½"

Making the Blocks

Each block is constructed using the pieces from one print and the ivory solid. Instructions are for making one block. Repeat to make a total of 30 blocks. Press all seam allowances in the direction indicated by the arrows. Before starting step 1, see "Triangle Paper for Scrap Call" on page 28.

1. Draw a diagonal line from corner to corner on the wrong side of the ivory 3" squares. Layer a marked square on a print 3" square, right sides together. Sew ¼" from both sides of the drawn line. Cut the unit apart on the marked line to make two half-square-triangle units. Make eight units. Trim the units to measure 2½" square, including seam allowances.

Make 8 units.

Triangle Paper for Scrap Call

I like to use half-square-triangle paper to make perfect units. For this quilt, I used Triangles on a Roll 2" finished-size half-square triangles. Instead of cutting ivory and print 3" squares, I cut 30 ivory 3¼" × 12½" rectangles and one 3¼" × 12½" rectangle from each print. If you choose this method, skip step 1 of "Making the Blocks" and follow the manufacturer's instructions to make eight half-square-triangle units from each print.

2. Join one ivory and one print 1½" × 25" strip along their long edges to make a strip set measuring 2½" × 25", including seam allowances. From the strip set, cut 16 segments, 1½" × 2½".

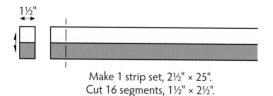

Make 1 strip set, 2½" × 25".
Cut 16 segments, 1½" × 2½".

3. Sew two segments together to make a four-patch unit. Make eight units measuring 2½" square, including seam allowances.

Make 8 units,
2½" × 2½".

4. Lay out two half-square-triangle units and two four-patch units in two rows as shown. Sew the units together into rows. Join the rows to make a corner unit. Make four units measuring 4½" square, including seam allowances.

Make 4 units,
4½" × 4½".

5. Lay out the corner units, four ivory 1½" × 4½" rectangles, and one print 1½" square in three rows, rotating the units as shown. Sew the pieces together into rows. Join the rows to make a block. Make 30 blocks measuring 9½" square, including seam allowances.

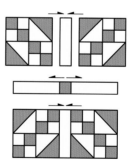 

Make 30 blocks,
9½" × 9½".

SCRAP CALL

2. When you're pleased with the arrangement, join four print squares to make a four-patch sashing unit. Make 20 units that measure 2½" square, including seam allowances. Return each unit to the appropriate position in the quilt layout.

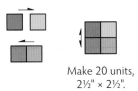

Make 20 units,
2½" × 2½".

3. Join two print squares to make a two-patch sashing unit. Make 18 units that measure 1½" × 2½", including seam allowances. Return each unit to the appropriate position in the quilt layout.

Make 18 units,
1½" × 2½".

4. Join two print 1½" squares, five aqua 1½" × 9½" rectangles, and four two-patch sashing units to make the top sashing row. The row should measure 1½" × 55½", including seam allowances. Repeat to make the bottom sashing row.

Make 2 rows, 1½" × 55½".

5. Join two aqua 1½" × 9½" rectangles, five blocks, and four aqua 2½" × 9½" rectangles to make a block row. Make six rows measuring 9½" × 55½", including seam allowances.

Make 6 rows, 9½" × 55½".

6. Join two two-patch sashing units, five aqua 2½" × 9½" rectangles, and four four-patch sashing units to make a sashing row. Make five rows measuring 2½" × 55½", including seam allowances.

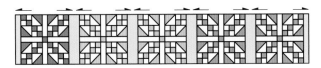

Make 5 rows, 2½" × 55½".

Assembling the Quilt Top

Refer to the photo on page 29 and the quilt assembly diagram on page 31 for placement guidance as needed throughout.

1. On a design wall, lay out the blocks in six rows of five blocks each. Place the aqua 2½" × 9½" rectangles between the blocks. Place the aqua 1½" × 9½" rectangles around the perimeter of the quilt layout. Pin four print 1½" squares between the aqua 2½"-wide rectangles to make four-patch sashing corners, making sure each square matches the corresponding block. Pin two print 1½" squares between the aqua rectangles along the sides, top, and bottom of the quilt center. Again, make sure each square matches the corresponding block. Using a square that matches the corner block, place a print 1½" square in each corner of the quilt layout.

7. Join the rows from steps 4–6 to complete the quilt-top center. The quilt top should measure 55½" × 66½", including seam allowances.

8. Join seven cream 2½"-wide strips end to end. From the pieced strip, cut two 66½"-long strips and two 59½"-long strips. Sew the longer strips to opposite sides of the quilt top. Sew the shorter strips to the top and bottom of the quilt top. Press all seam allowances toward the cream strips. The quilt top should measure 59½" × 70½".

Finishing the Quilt

For more details on any finishing steps, visit ShopMartingale.com/HowtoQuilt for free downloadable information.

1. Prepare the quilt backing so it's about 6" larger in both directions than the quilt top.

2. Layer the quilt top with batting and backing; baste the layers together.

3. Quilt by hand or machine. The quilt shown is machine quilted with an allover floral design.

4. Use the remaining cream 2½"-wide strips to make the binding; attach the binding to the quilt.

Quilt assembly

Counting Stars

FINISHED QUILT
48½" × 48½"

FINISHED BLOCKS
12" × 12" and
6" × 12"

There's something about a chain in a quilt that makes my heart beat a little faster—especially when that chain is scrappy. The green Sprouts bundle was the perfect backdrop to a little Christmas in my life. When I added a few more green prints, one red print, and a background print, a fun playday began. This design is called Counting Stars because every time I left the sewing machine, I would come back and ask myself, "How many stars do I need?" But the best part of this quilt—and the most fun—is that the borders are stitched right into the rows, so you don't need to assemble the blocks and then add the borders.

Materials

Yardage is based on 42"-wide fabric. Fat eighths measure 9" × 21".

21 fat eighths of assorted green prints for blocks*
1⅛ yards of cream print for blocks
2½ yards of red print for blocks and binding
3⅛ yards of fabric for backing
55" × 55" piece of batting

In place of some of the assorted green fat eighths, I used Sprouts Color Cuts in the Dessert Roll size.

Cutting

All measurements include ¼" seam allowances.

From *each of 5* green prints, cut:
4 squares, 4" × 4" (20 total)
1 square, 2½" × 2½" (5 total)
8 squares, 1½" × 1½" (40 total)

From the *remaining 16* green prints, cut a *total* of:
1 strip, 2½" × 21"
11 strips, 1½" × 21"
80 squares, 1½" × 1½"

From the cream print, cut:
2 strips, 4" × 42"; crosscut the strips into
    20 squares, 4" × 4"
3 strips, 3½" × 42"; crosscut the strips into
    28 squares, 3½" × 3½"
12 strips, 1½" × 42"; crosscut the strips into:
    16 strips, 1½" × 10½"
    16 strips, 1½" × 6½"
    20 rectangles, 1½" × 2½"
    52 squares, 1½" × 1½"

Continued on page 34

Continued from page 33

From the red print, cut:

1 strip, 6½" × 42"; crosscut the strip into 4 squares, 6½" × 6½"

2 strips, 5½" × 42"; crosscut the strips into 3 strips, 5½" × 21"

4 strips, 4½" × 42"; crosscut the strips into:
  5 strips, 4½" × 21"
  10 rectangles, 1½" × 4½"

3 strips, 3½" × 42"; crosscut the strips into:
  4 strips, 3½" × 21"
  8 squares, 3½" × 3½"

9 strips, 2½" × 42"; crosscut *3 of the strips* into:
  4 strips, 2½" × 21"
  4 squares, 2½" × 2½"

9 strips, 1½" × 42"; crosscut the strips into:
  4 strips, 1½" × 21"
  16 rectangles, 1½" × 8½"
  18 rectangles, 1½" × 6½"

Making Block A

Press all seam allowances in the direction indicated by the arrows.

1. Draw a diagonal line from corner to corner on the wrong side of the green 1½" squares. Place a marked square on one end of a cream 1½" × 2½" rectangle, right sides together. Sew on the marked line. Trim the excess corner fabric ¼" from the stitched line. Place a matching green square on the opposite end of the cream rectangle. Sew and trim as before to make a flying-geese unit. Make five sets of four matching units (20 total). The units should measure 1½" × 2½", including seam allowances.

Make 5 sets of
4 matching units,
1½" × 2½".

2. Lay out four cream 1½" squares, four matching flying-geese units, and one matching green 2½" square in three rows. Sew the squares and units together into rows. Join the rows to make a star unit. Make five units measuring 4½" square, including seam allowances.

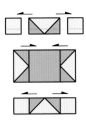

Make 5 units,
4½" × 4½".

3. Sew red 1½" × 4½" rectangles to opposite sides of a star unit. Sew red 1½" × 6½" rectangles to the top and bottom of the unit to make a center unit. Make five units measuring 6½" square, including seam allowances.

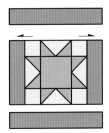 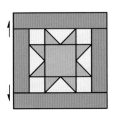

Make 5 units,
6½" × 6½".

4. Draw a diagonal line from corner to corner on the wrong side of the cream 4" squares. Layer a marked square on a green 4" square, right sides together. Sew ¼" from both sides of the drawn line. Cut the unit apart on the marked line to make two half-square-triangle units. On one unit, press the seam allowances toward the green triangle. On the other unit, press the seam allowances toward the cream triangle. Make five sets of eight matching units (40 total). Trim the units to measure 3½" square, including seam allowances.

3½"

3½"

Make 5 sets of
8 matching units.

Making Block B

1. Join two cream 1½" squares and two green 1½" squares to make a four-patch unit. Make 16 units measuring 2½" square, including seam allowances.

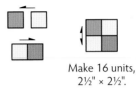

Make 16 units,
2½" × 2½".

2. Draw a diagonal line from corner to corner on the wrong side of the remaining cream 3½" squares. Layer a marked square on a red 3½" square, right sides together. Repeat step 4 of "Making Block A" on page 34 to make 16 half-square-triangle units measuring 3⅛" square, including seam allowances.

3. On the wrong side of eight units, draw a diagonal line from corner to corner, perpendicular to the seamline. Place two units right sides together. Make sure contrasting fabrics are facing each other and the marked square is on top. Nest the seam allowances against each other and stitch ¼" from both sides of the marked line. Cut the units apart on the drawn line to make two hourglass units. Make 16 units. Trim the units to measure 2½" square, including seam allowances.

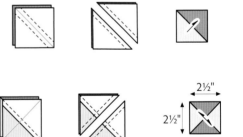

Make 16 units.

5. Join two matching half-square-triangle units, with the seam allowances pressed in the opposite directions, to make a side unit. Make five sets of four matching units (20 total) that measure 3½" × 6½", including seam allowances.

Make 5 sets of
4 matching units,
3½" × 6½".

6. Lay out four cream 3½" squares, four matching side units, and one center unit from the same green print in three rows as shown. Sew the squares and units together into rows. Join the rows to make block A. Make five of block A. The blocks should measure 12½" square, including seam allowances.

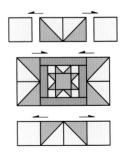
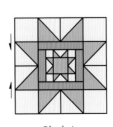

Block A.
Make 5 blocks,
12½" × 12½".

4. Lay out four four-patch units, four hourglass units, and one red 2½" square in three rows, rotating the units as shown. Sew the units and squares together into rows. Join the rows to make an Ohio Star unit. Make four units measuring 6½" square, including seam allowances.

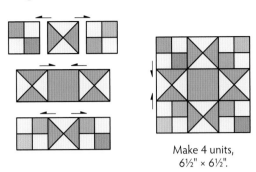

Make 4 units,
6½" × 6½".

5. Sew cream 1½" × 6½" rectangles to opposite sides of an Ohio Star unit. Sew green 1½" squares to the ends of two cream 1½" × 6½" rectangles and sew the pieced rectangles to the top and bottom of the unit. Make four units measuring 8½" square, including seam allowances.

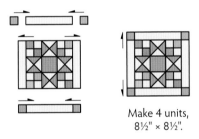

Make 4 units,
8½" × 8½".

6. Sew red 1½" × 8½" rectangles to opposite sides of a unit from step 5. Sew green 1½" squares to the ends of two red 1½" × 8½" rectangles and sew them to the top and bottom of the unit. Make four units measuring 10½" square, including seam allowances.

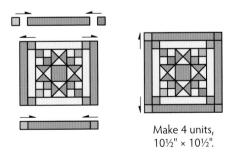

Make 4 units,
10½" × 10½".

7. Sew cream 1½" × 10½" rectangles to opposite sides of a unit. Sew green 1½" squares to the ends of two cream 1½" × 10½" rectangles and sew them to the top and bottom of the block. Make four of block B. The blocks should measure 12½" square, including seam allowances.

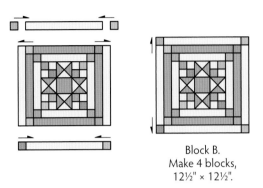

Block B.
Make 4 blocks,
12½" × 12½".

Making Blocks C and D

1. Join a green 1½" × 21" strip and a red 5½" × 21" strip along their long edges to make a strip set. Make three strip sets measuring 6½" × 21", including seam allowances. From two of the strip sets, cut 24 A segments, 1½" × 6½". From the remaining strip set, cut eight B segments, 2½" × 6½".

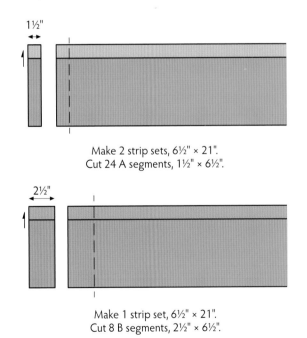

1½"

Make 2 strip sets, 6½" × 21".
Cut 24 A segments, 1½" × 6½".

2½"

Make 1 strip set, 6½" × 21".
Cut 8 B segments, 2½" × 6½".

2. Join a red 1½" × 21" strip, a green 1½" × 21" strip, and a red 4½" × 21" strip along their long edges to make a strip set. Make four strip sets measuring 6½" × 21", including seam allowances. From the strip sets, cut 40 C segments, 1½" × 6½".

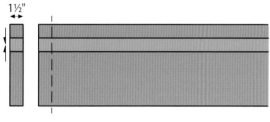

Make 4 strip sets, 6½" × 21".
Cut 40 C segments, 1½" × 6½".

3. Join a red 2½" × 21" strip, a green 1½" × 21" strip, and a red 3½" × 21" strip along their long edges to make a strip set. Make four strip sets measuring 6½" × 21", including seam allowances. From the strip sets, cut 48 D segments, 1½" × 6½".

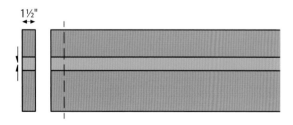

Make 4 strip sets, 6½" × 21".
Cut 48 D segments, 1½" × 6½".

4. Join a green 2½" × 21" strip and a red 4½" × 21" strip along their long edges to make one strip set measuring 6½" × 21", including seam allowances. From the strip set, cut four E segments, 2½" × 6½".

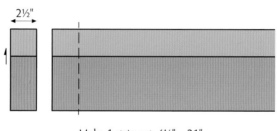

Make 1 strip set, 6½" × 21".
Cut 4 E segments, 2½" × 6½".

5. Join two A, one B, four C, and four D segments as shown to make block C. Make eight blocks measuring 6½" × 12½", including seam allowances.

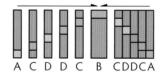

A C D D C B C D D C A

Block C.
Make 8 blocks,
6½" × 12½".

6. Join two A, two C, four D, and one E segment. Add a red 1½" × 6½" rectangle to each end to make block D. Make four blocks measuring 6½" × 12½", including seam allowances.

A C D D E D D C A

Block D.
Make 4 blocks,
6½" × 12½".

Assembling the Quilt Top

Instead of piecing the blocks and borders separately, assemble the entire quilt in five horizontal rows. This way there's less chance of error than if you piece the side borders first and then attach them to the quilt center.

1. Lay out the A–D blocks and four red 6½" squares in five rows as shown in the quilt assembly diagram below.

2. Sew the blocks and squares together into rows. Join the rows to complete the quilt top, which should measure 48½" square.

Finishing the Quilt

For more details on any finishing steps, visit ShopMartingale.com/HowtoQuilt for free downloadable information.

1. Prepare the quilt backing so it's about 6" larger in both directions than the quilt top.

2. Layer the quilt top with batting and backing; baste the layers together.

3. Quilt by hand or machine. The quilt shown is machine quilted with an allover design of swirls and stars.

4. Use the remaining red 2½"-wide strips to make the binding; attach the binding to the quilt.

Quilt assembly

Sprinkle with Pepper

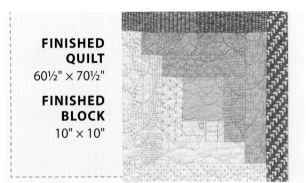

FINISHED QUILT
60½" × 70½"

FINISHED BLOCK
10" × 10"

Indecision is the real reason that this is my very first Log Cabin quilt—uncertainty about the size of logs to cut, the color of the center square (since they all have a different meaning), and finally, the setting. OK, along comes the Color Cuts Road Trip bundle—those grays were just the push I needed to make my very first Log Cabin quilt. I found a perfect yellow for the center, which also means a light in the window to say, "Welcome home." For the logs, I selected some of my prettiest putzy white backgrounds and little bits of grays, along with those Road Trip grays. Since I'd never made a Log Cabin before, a 10" block seemed easy to accomplish. The number of blocks also let me play with a fun setting, and believe me, that's the part I wanted to get to as fast as I could.

Materials

Yardage is based on 42"-wide fabric.

1 yard of yellow solid for blocks and binding
2½ yards *total* of cream prints for blocks
3⅛ yards *total* of gray prints for blocks*
3¾ yards of fabric for backing
67" × 77" piece of batting

I used a fat-quarter bundle of Road Trip Color Cuts in place of the gray yardage.

Cutting

All measurements include ¼" seam allowances.

From the yellow solid, cut:
4 strips, 3" × 42"; crosscut the strips into
    42 squares, 3" × 3"
7 strips, 2½" × 42"

From the cream prints, cut a *total* of:
42 rectangles, 1¾" × 3" (A)
42 rectangles, 1¾" × 4¼" (B)
42 rectangles, 1¾" × 5½" (E)
42 rectangles, 1¾" × 6¾" (F)
42 rectangles, 1¾" × 8" (I)
42 rectangles, 1¾" × 9¼" (J)

From the gray prints, cut a *total* of:
42 rectangles, 1¾" × 4¼" (C)
42 rectangles, 1¾" × 5½" (D)
42 rectangles, 1¾" × 6¾" (G)
42 rectangles, 1¾" × 8" (H)
42 rectangles, 1¾" × 9¼" (K)
42 rectangles, 1¾" × 10½" (L)

41

Making the Blocks

Press all seam allowances in the direction indicated by the arrows.

1. Sew a cream A rectangle to the left side of a yellow square. Sew a cream B rectangle to the top of the square. Sew a gray C rectangle to the right side and a gray D rectangle to the bottom of the square to make a center unit. Make 42 units measuring 5½" square, including seam allowances.

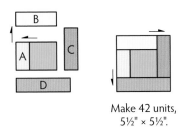

Make 42 units,
5½" × 5½".

2. Sew a cream E rectangle to the left side of the center unit. Add a cream F, a gray G, and a gray H rectangle to the unit. Make 42 units measuring 8" square, including seam allowances.

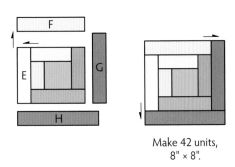

Make 42 units,
8" × 8".

3. Sew a cream I rectangle to the left side of the unit from step 2. Add a cream J, a gray K, and a gray L rectangle to complete a block. Make 42 blocks measuring 10½" square, including seam allowances.

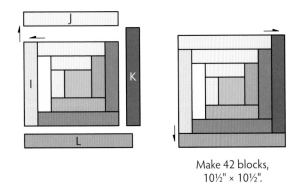

Make 42 blocks,
10½" × 10½".

Assembling the Quilt Top

Lay out the blocks in seven rows of six blocks each, rotating them as shown in the quilt assembly diagram below. Sew the blocks together into rows. Join the rows to complete the quilt top, which should measure 60½" × 70½".

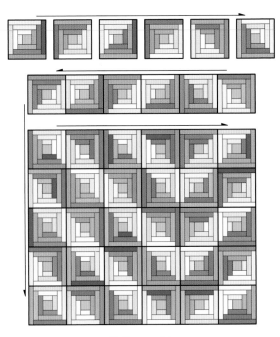

Quilt assembly

Finishing the Quilt

For more details on any finishing steps, visit ShopMartingale.com/HowtoQuilt for free downloadable information.

1. Prepare the quilt backing so it's about 6" larger in both directions than the quilt top.

2. Layer the quilt top with batting and backing; baste the layers together.

3. Quilt by hand or machine. The quilt shown is machine quilted with an allover design of ovals.

4. Use the yellow 2½"-wide strips to make the binding; attach the binding to the quilt.

43

Dot, Dot, Dot

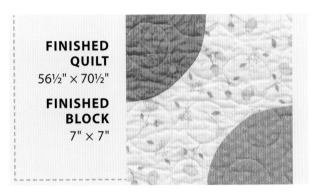

FINISHED QUILT
56½" × 70½"

FINISHED BLOCK
7" × 7"

The quilting world may call backgrounds in neutral colors low volume, *but I've called them putzy prints since my very first quilt. There's nothing cuter than tons of little white and off-white printed fabrics piled up ready for a quilt. How much more fun can you add to that except for the dots? I just happened to have two great reds that were close to one another in color and style to give the dots some extra pizzazz. But honestly, I could remake this quilt using just about any color of dots and be just as happy. Start with a Color Cuts bundle of Sugar on Top and a bit of gentle curved piecing, and soon you'll have your own Dot, Dot, Dot.*

Materials

Yardage is based on 42"-wide fabric. Fat quarters measure 18" × 21".

20 fat quarters of assorted light prints for blocks*
1¼ yards of red print #1 for blocks
1¾ yards of red print #2 for blocks and binding
3½ yards of fabric for backing
63" × 77" piece of batting
Template plastic or cardstock

**I used a Color Cuts ½-yard bundle of Sugar on Top in place of the fat quarters.*

Cutting

All measurements include ¼" seam allowances.

From red print #1, cut:
9 strips, 4¼" × 42"

From red print #2, cut:
9 strips, 4¼" × 42"
7 strips, 2½" × 42"

Making the Blocks

Press all seam allowances in the direction indicated by the arrows.

1. Trace the A and B patterns on pages 48 and 49 onto template plastic or cardstock and cut out the templates on the drawn lines.

2. Use template A to cut four shapes from each light print (80 total). If you're using half-yard cuts, cut eight shapes from each of 10 prints. Use template B and the red 4¼"-wide strips to cut 80 shapes from each red print (160 total).

3. Fold a light A piece in half and lightly crease to mark the center of the curved edges. In the same way, mark the center on the curved edge of a red #1 and a red #2 B piece. Pin the A piece on top of the red #1 B piece, matching the centers and ends, and sew along the curved edges. Repeat to sew the red #2 B piece to the other curved edge of the A piece to make a block. Make 80 blocks measuring 7½" square, including seam allowances.

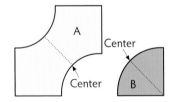

Make 80 blocks,
7½" × 7½".

Assembling the Quilt Top

Lay out the blocks in 10 rows of eight blocks each, rotating the blocks as shown in the quilt assembly diagram below to create red circles. Sew the blocks together into rows. Join the rows to complete the quilt top, which should measure 56½" × 70½".

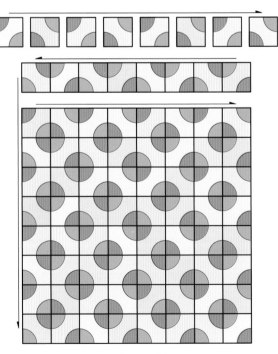

Quilt assembly

47
DOT, DOT, DOT

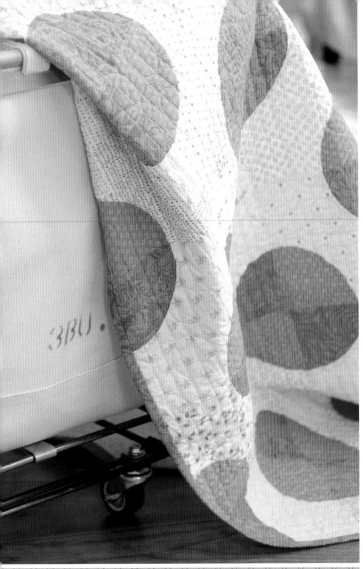

Finishing the Quilt

For more details on any finishing steps, visit ShopMartingale.com/HowtoQuilt for free downloadable information.

1. Prepare the quilt backing so it's about 6" larger in both directions than the quilt top.

2. Layer the quilt top with batting and backing; baste the layers together.

3. Quilt by hand or machine. The quilt shown is machine quilted with an allover design of parallel vertical lines and circles.

4. Use the red 2½"-wide strips to make the binding; attach the binding to the quilt.

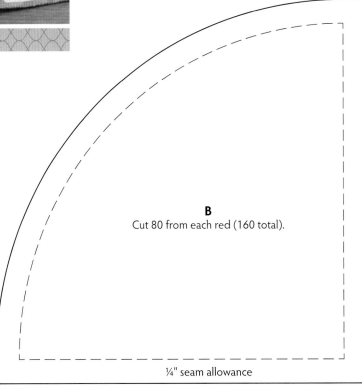

B
Cut 80 from each red (160 total).

¼" seam allowance

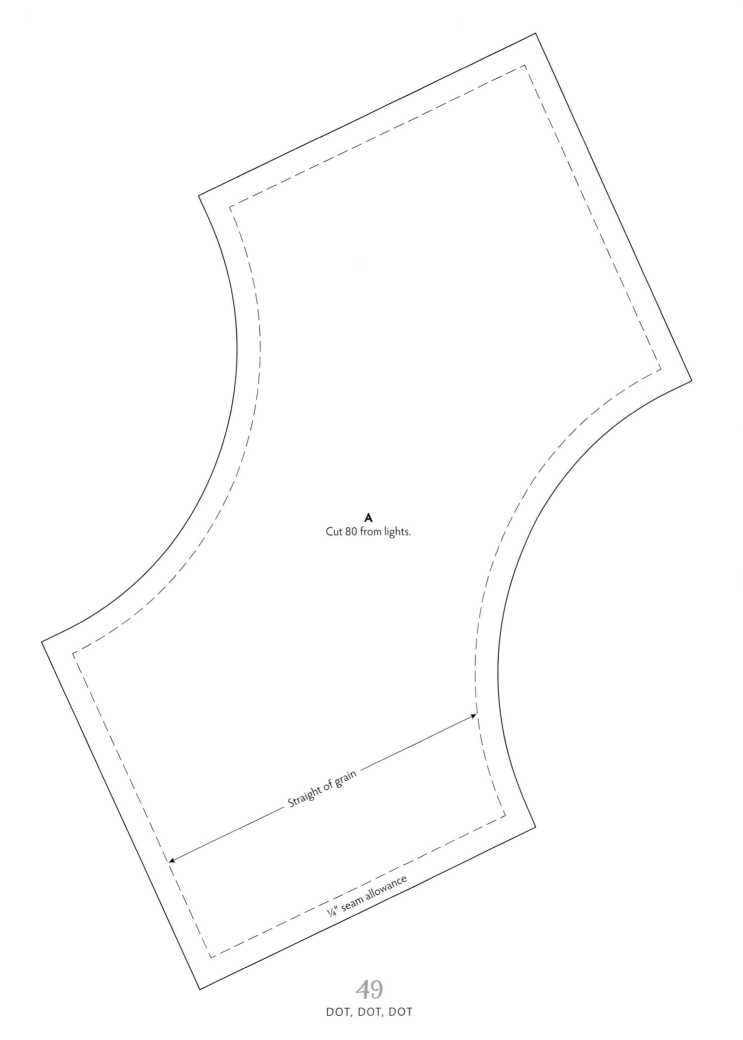

A
Cut 80 from lights.

Straight of grain

¼" seam allowance

49

Chiclets and Gumballs

FINISHED QUILT
53½" × 53½"

FINISHED BLOCKS
5" × 5"

a t the beginning of summer, I pull out my scrap bins and start making little blocks just to play. A few years ago, I played with little 25-Patch blocks and some appliquéd circles, and the Chiclets and Gumballs quilt was born. The minute I saw all the colors of Color Cuts, the fabric was screaming at me to remake my scrap-bin version. I used every color, and to top it all off, I added a few more light background prints to make it more fun!

Materials

Yardage is based on 42"-wide fabric.

⅝ yard *total* of assorted teal prints for blocks and pieced border*

⅝ yard *total* of assorted gray prints for blocks and pieced border*

⅝ yard *total* of assorted pink prints for blocks and pieced border*

⅝ yard *total* of assorted green prints for blocks and pieced border*

½ yard *total* of assorted yellow prints for blocks and pieced border*

1¾ yards *total* of assorted cream prints for blocks and pieced border

1¾ yards of white print for blocks, borders, and binding

3½ yards of fabric for backing

60" × 60" piece of batting

½ yard of 20"-wide lightweight interfacing

Template plastic or cardstock

You can use 10"-square Color Cut bundles in place of the assorted teal, gray, pink, green, and yellow yardage.

Cutting

All measurements include ¼" seam allowances.

From the assorted teal prints, cut a *total* of:
18 rectangles, 1½" × 10"
2 squares, 5" × 5"

From *each of 2* teal prints, cut:
2 squares, 3" × 3"; cut the squares in half diagonally to yield 4 C triangles (8 total)
1 square, 5½" × 5½"; cut the square into quarters diagonally to yield 4 D triangles (8 total)

From the assorted gray prints, cut a *total* of:
18 rectangles, 1½" × 10"
2 squares, 5" × 5"

From *each of 2* gray prints, cut:
2 squares, 3" × 3"; cut the squares in half diagonally to yield 4 C triangles (8 total)
1 square, 5½" × 5½"; cut the square into quarters diagonally to yield 4 D triangles (8 total)

From the assorted pink prints, cut a *total* of:
18 rectangles, 1½" × 10"
2 squares, 5" × 5"

Continued on page 52

Continued from page 51

From *each of 2* pink prints, cut:

2 squares, 3" × 3"; cut the squares in half diagonally to yield 4 C triangles (8 total)

1 square, 5½" × 5½"; cut the square into quarters diagonally to yield 4 D triangles (8 total)

From the assorted green prints, cut a *total* of:

18 rectangles, 1½" × 10"

2 squares, 5" × 5"

From *each of 2* green prints, cut:

2 squares, 3" × 3"; cut the squares in half diagonally to yield 4 C triangles (8 total)

1 square, 5½" × 5½"; cut the square into quarters diagonally to yield 4 D triangles (8 total)

From the assorted yellow prints, cut a *total* of:

10 rectangles, 1½" × 10"

1 square, 5" × 5"

From *1* yellow print, cut:

2 squares, 3" × 3"; cut the squares in half diagonally to yield 4 C triangles

1 square, 5½" × 5½"; cut the square into quarters diagonally to yield 4 D triangles

From the remaining teal, gray, pink, green, and yellow prints, cut a *total* of:

176 rectangles, 1½" × 3½"

8 rectangles, 1½" × 2½"

8 squares, 1½" × 1½"

From the assorted cream prints, cut a *total* of:

78 rectangles, 1½" × 10"

9 squares, 5½" × 5½"

176 squares, 1½" × 1½"

From the white print, cut:

15 strips, 1½" × 42"; crosscut the strips into:

    4 rectangles, 1½" × 7½"

    52 rectangles, 1½" × 5½"

    20 rectangles, 1½" × 4½"

    32 rectangles, 1½" × 3½"

    12 squares, 1½" × 1½"

6 strips, 2½" × 42"

6 strips, 2" × 42"

5 strips, 1¼" × 42"

From the interfacing, cut:

9 squares, 5" × 5"

Making the 25-Patch Blocks

Press all seam allowances in the direction indicated by the arrows.

1. Join three teal and two cream 1½" × 10" rectangles along their long edges to make a strip set. Make four strip sets measuring 5½" × 10", including seam allowances. From the strip sets, cut 24 A segments, 1½" × 5½".

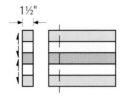

Make 4 strip sets, 5½" × 10".
Cut 24 A segments, 1½" × 5½".

2. Repeat step 1 to make four strip sets of each colorway: pink/cream, green/cream, and gray/cream. Cut 24 A segments from each color combination. Make two yellow/cream strip sets and cut 12 A segments.

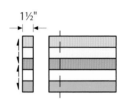

Make 4 strip sets, 5½" × 10".
Cut 24 A segments, 1½" × 5½".

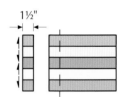

Make 4 strip sets, 5½" × 10".
Cut 24 A segments, 1½" × 5½".

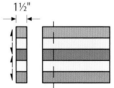

Make 4 strip sets, 5½" × 10".
Cut 24 A segments, 1½" × 5½".

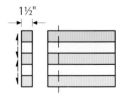

Make 2 strip sets, 5½" × 10".
Cut 12 A segments, 1½" × 5½".

3. Join three cream and two teal 1½" × 10" rectangles along their long edges to make a strip set. Make three strip sets measuring 5½" × 10", including seam allowances. From the strip sets, cut 16 B segments, 1½" × 5½". Repeat to make three strip sets each using gray/cream, pink/cream, and

green/cream. Cut 16 B segments from each color combination. Make two yellow/cream strip sets and cut eight B segments.

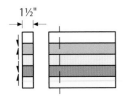

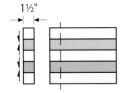
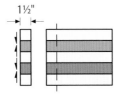

Make 3 strip sets, 5½" × 10".
Cut 16 B segments, 1½" × 5½".

Make 3 strip sets, 5½" × 10".
Cut 16 B segments, 1½" × 5½".

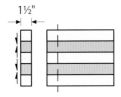

Make 3 strip sets, 5½" × 10".
Cut 16 B segments, 1½" × 5½".

Make 3 strip sets, 5½" × 10".
Cut 16 B segments, 1½" × 5½".

Make 2 strip sets, 5½" × 10".
Cut 8 B segments, 1½" × 5½".

4. Lay out three A and two B segments for each colorway, starting and ending with an A segment. Join the segments to make a 25-Patch block. Make eight teal, gray, pink, and green blocks. Make four yellow blocks. The blocks should measure 5½" square, including seam allowances.

Make 8 blocks,
5½" × 5½".

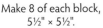

Make 8 of each block,
5½" × 5½".

Make 4 blocks,
5½" × 5½".

Making the Appliquéd Blocks

1. Trace the circle pattern on page 58 onto template plastic or cardstock and cut out the template on the drawn line. Use the template to draw a circle on each square of interfacing.

2. Place the interfacing square on the right side of a teal 5" square, with the marked circle on top. Sewing on the marked line, stitch around the circle, making sure to start and stop with a backstitch.

Machine stitch directly
on traced line.

3. Cut out the circle ⅛" beyond the stitched line. Carefully make a slit through the center of the interfacing layer. Make little snips in the seam allowance around the perimeter of the circle. Turn the circle inside out through the slit.

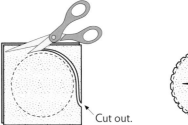

Clip.

Slit

Cut out.

4. To make crisp edges, use a knitting needle or chopstick on the inside of the shape to gently press into the seams. Take your time, being careful to not rip a hole in the seam. Press the circle on the front.

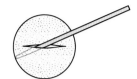

Glide back and forth
on inside of seam gently
for crisp edge.

5. Center a circle on the right side of a cream 5½" square. Appliqué by hand or machine. Make two teal, gray, pink, and green blocks and one yellow block. The blocks should measure 5½" square, including seam allowances.

Make 2 of each block,
5½" × 5½".

Make 1 block,
5½" × 5½".

Making the Setting Blocks and Triangles

After making each setting block or triangle, return it to its position on the design wall.

1. Before making the setting blocks, side triangles, and corner triangles, lay out the 25-Patch blocks and appliquéd blocks on a design wall so you can match the colors used in the adjacent blocks. Place the

25-Patch blocks in an on-point grid of six blocks by six blocks. Add the appliquéd blocks, matching the colors to the surrounding blocks.

Lay out blocks

2. Pin four C triangles to the corners of each corresponding block on the design wall. Pin four D triangles to the sides of each corresponding block.

3. Where four C triangles adjoin in the quilt layout, join them to make an hourglass unit measuring 3½" square, including seam allowances. Sew white 1½" × 3½" rectangles to opposite sides of the unit. Sew white 1½" × 5½" rectangles to the top and

bottom of the unit to make a C setting block. Make four blocks measuring 5½" square, including seam allowances. Place the blocks back in the quilt layout.

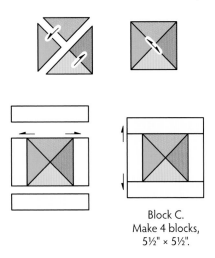

Block C.
Make 4 blocks,
5½" × 5½".

4. Where two D triangles are arranged side by side, join them along their long edges to make a half-square-triangle unit measuring 3½" square, including seam allowances. Sew white 1½" × 3½" rectangles to opposite sides of the unit. Sew white 1½" × 5½" rectangles to the top and bottom of the unit to make a D setting block. Make 12 blocks measuring 5½" square, including seam allowances. Place the blocks back in the quilt layout.

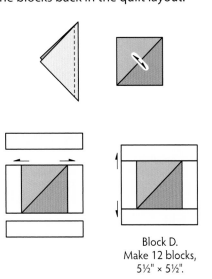

Block D.
Make 12 blocks,
5½" × 5½".

5. Where two C triangles are side by side in the layout, join them along their short sides to make a triangle unit. Sew a white 1½" × 4½" rectangle to one short side of the unit. Sew a white 1½" × 5½" rectangle to the adjacent side of the unit to make a C side setting triangle. Make eight.

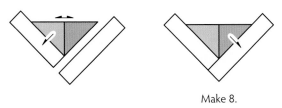

Make 8.

6. Sew a white 1½" × 4½" rectangle to one short side of a D triangle. Sew a white 1½" × 5½" rectangle to the adjacent side of the triangle to make a D side setting triangle. Make 12.

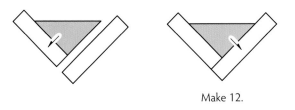

Make 12.

7. Sew a white 1½" × 7½" rectangle to the long side of a C triangle to make a corner setting triangle. Make four.

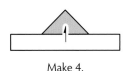

Make 4.

Assembling the Quilt Top

1. Referring to the quilt assembly diagram below, sew together the pieces in each diagonal row. Join the rows and add the corner triangles and the C and D side setting triangles.

Quilt assembly

2. Trim the quilt top to measure 43" square, including seam allowances, making sure to leave ¼" beyond the points on all of the blocks for seam allowances.

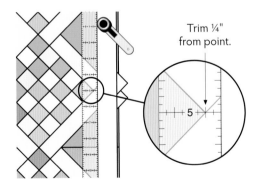

Trim ¼" from point.

Making the Pieced Border

1. Draw a diagonal line from corner to corner on the wrong side of the cream 1½" squares. Place a marked square on one end of a print 1½" × 3½" rectangle,

right sides together. Sew on the marked line. Trim the excess corner fabric, ¼" from the stitched line. Make 88 units and 88 mirror-imaged units.

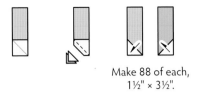

Make 88 of each, 1½" × 3½".

2. Join the units and mirror-imaged units in pairs to make 88 units measuring 2½" × 3½".

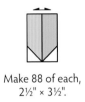

Make 88 of each, 2½" × 3½".

3. Join two white 1½" squares and two print squares to make a four-patch unit measuring 2½" square, including seam allowances. Sew the four-patch unit, two print 1½" × 2½" rectangles, and one white 1½" square together into rows. Join the rows to make a corner block. Make four blocks measuring 3½" square, including seam allowances.

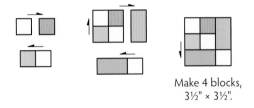

Make 4 blocks, 3½" × 3½".

4. Join 22 units from step 2 to make a side border measuring 3½" × 44½", including seam allowances. Make four and press the seam allowances open. Add a corner block to each end of two borders, rotating the blocks as shown. These borders should measure 3½" × 50½", including seam allowances.

Make 2 side borders, 3½" × 44½".

Make 2 top/bottom borders, 3½" × 50½".

Adding the Borders

1. Join the white 1¼" strips end to end. From the pieced strip, cut two 44½"-long strips and two 43"-long strips. Sew the shorter strips to the sides of the quilt top. Sew the longer strips to the top and bottom edges. The quilt top should measure 44½" square, including seam allowances.

2. Sew two pieced borders to the sides of the quilt top, and then sew two to the top and bottom of the quilt top, which should measure 50½" square, including seam allowances.

3. Join the white 2"-wide strips end to end. From the pieced strip, cut two 53½"-long strips and two 50½"-long strips. Sew the shorter strips to the sides of the quilt top. Sew the longer strips to the top and bottom edges of the quilt top, which should measure 53½" square.

Finishing the Quilt

For more details on any finishing steps, visit ShopMartingale.com/HowtoQuilt for free downloadable information.

1. Prepare the quilt backing so it's about 6" larger in both directions than the quilt top.

2. Layer the quilt top with batting and backing; baste the layers together.

3. Quilt by hand or machine. The quilt shown is machine quilted with an allover design of vertical lines and circles.

4. Use the white 2½"-wide strips to make the binding; attach the binding to the quilt.

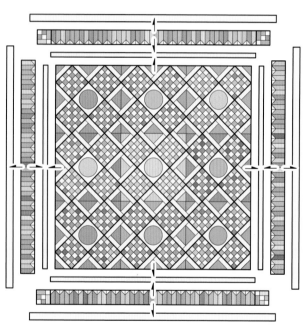

Adding borders

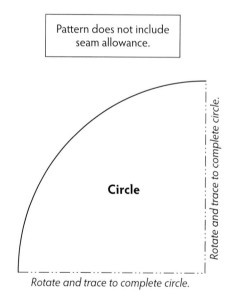

Pattern does not include seam allowance.

Circle

Rotate and trace to complete circle.

Rotate and trace to complete circle.

Pink-Tie Party

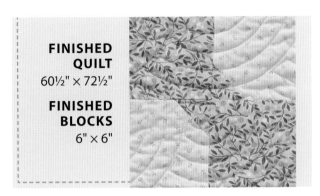

FINISHED QUILT
60½" × 72½"

FINISHED BLOCKS
6" × 6"

I collected quilts even before I knew that quilt blocks had names. In my foraging for the cute, I stumbled across a sad, ripped, and worn pink Bow Tie quilt. To this day, it's still one of my very favorite quilts, even though the batting barely exists and most of the backgrounds are disappearing with age. Maybe the pinks were originally red, but I'll call the quilt pink and blue forever, and it will always be in my collection. What better way to use Daybreak Color Cuts than to re-create some vintage fun!

Materials

Yardage is based on 42"-wide fabric. Fat quarters measure 18" × 21". Fat eighths measure 9" × 21".

12 fat quarters of assorted pink prints for blocks*
17 fat eighths of assorted light prints for blocks
3⅛ yards of blue print for setting squares, border, and binding
3¾ yards of fabric for backing
67" × 79" piece of batting

I used a fat-quarter Color Cuts bundle in Daybreak for the pink prints.

Cutting

All measurements include ¼" seam allowances.

From *10* pink prints, cut:
8 squares, 3½" × 3½" (80 total)
8 squares, 1¾" × 1¾" (80 total)

From the *remaining 2* pink prints, cut:
10 squares, 3½" × 3½" (20 total)
10 squares, 1¾" × 1¾" (20 total)

From the light prints, cut a *total* of:
50 pairs of matching squares, 3½" × 3½"

From the blue print, cut:
9 strips, 6½" × 42"; crosscut the strips into
    49 squares, 6½" × 6½"
7 strips, 3½" × 42"
7 strips, 2½" × 42"

Making the Blocks

Press all seam allowances in the direction indicated by the arrows.

1. Draw a diagonal line from corner to corner on the wrong side of the pink 1¾" squares. Place a marked square on one corner of a light 3½" square. Sew on the marked line. Trim the excess corner fabric ¼" from the stitched line. Make 50 pairs of matching units (100 units total). The units should measure 3½" square, including seam allowances.

Make 100 units,
3½" × 3½".

59

2. Using pink 3½" squares that match the units from step 1, lay out two units and two pink squares in two rows of two. Sew the pieces together into rows. Join the rows to make a block. Make 50 blocks measuring 6½" square, including seam allowances.

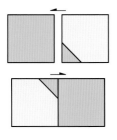 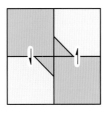

Make 50 blocks,
6½" × 6½".

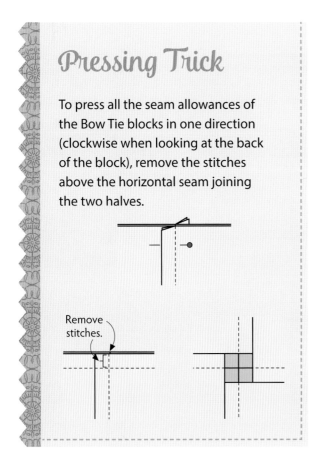

Pressing Trick

To press all the seam allowances of the Bow Tie blocks in one direction (clockwise when looking at the back of the block), remove the stitches above the horizontal seam joining the two halves.

Remove
stitches.

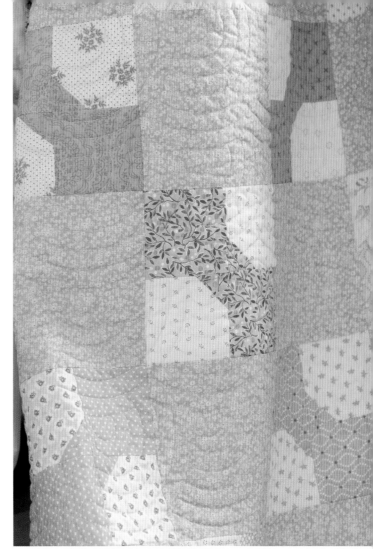

Assembling the Quilt Top

1. Lay out the blocks and blue squares in 11 rows, alternating the blocks and squares in each row and from row to row as shown in the quilt assembly diagram below. Sew the blocks and squares together into rows. Join the rows to make the quilt center, which should measure 54½" × 66½", including seam allowances.

2. Join the blue 3½"-wide strips end to end. From the pieced strip, cut two 66½"-long strips and two 60½"-long strips. Sew the longer strips to opposite sides of the quilt top. Sew the shorter strips to the top and bottom of the quilt top, which should measure 60½" × 72½".

Finishing the Quilt

For more details on any finishing steps, visit ShopMartingale.com/HowtoQuilt for free downloadable information.

1. Prepare the quilt backing so it's about 6" larger in both directions than the quilt top.

2. Layer the quilt top with batting and backing; baste the layers together.

3. Quilt by hand or machine. The quilt shown is machine quilted with an allover Baptist fan design.

4. Use the blue 2½"-wide strips to make the binding; attach the binding to the quilt.

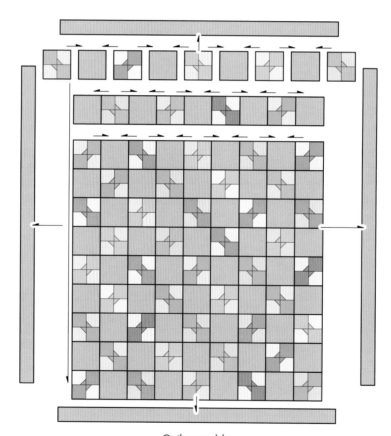

Quilt assembly

63

PINK-TIE PARTY

About the Author

Knowing only that she wanted to feature embroidery and Nine Patch blocks, Susan Ache taught herself to make her first quilt. Quiltmaking opened up a new world to this mom of five now-grown children. She turned many hours reading about quiltmaking into a lifelong passion for creating beautiful quilts.

Susan finds color inspiration in her native Florida surroundings. She's always searching for new and fun ways to show off as many colors as she can in a quilt. Most of her quilts are a creative impulse inspired by a trip to the garden center, a photograph in a magazine, or a few paint color swatches. She never sees just the quilt—she sees the room where the quilt belongs.

Working in a quilt store for years helped cultivate Susan's love of color and fabric. Visit Susan on Pinterest and Instagram as @yardgrl60.

Acknowledgment

Special thanks to long-arm quilter Susan Rogers, who beautifully quilted all of the projects in this book.